WANTED!

— FAMOUS OUTLAWS —

NED KELLY

A NOTORIOUS BANDIT OF THE AUSTRALIAN OUTBACK

TIM COOKE

Gareth Stevens
PUBLISHING

Please visit our website, **www.garethstevens.com**.
For a free color catalog of all our high-quality books,
call toll-free 1-800-542-2595 or fax 1-877-542-2596.

Library of Congress Cataloging-in-Publication Data

Cooke, Tim, 1961-
 Ned Kelly : a notorious bandit of the Australian outback / Tim Cooke.
    pages cm. — (Wanted! Famous outlaws)
 Includes index and bibliographical references.
 ISBN 978-1-4824-4266-3 (pbk.)
 ISBN 978-1-4824-4267-0 (6 pack)
 ISBN 978-1-4824-4262-5 (library binding)
 1. Kelly, Ned, 1855-1880—Juvenile literature. 2. Bushrangers—Australia—Biography—Juvenile literature.
 3. Outlaws—Australia—Biography—Juvenile literature. 4. Kelly family—Juvenile literature.
 5. Irish—Australia—Victoria—Biography—Juvenile literature. I. Title.
 DU222.K4C66 2016
 364.15'5092—dc23
 [B]

                        2015029226

Published in 2016 by
Gareth Stevens Publishing
111 East 14th Street, Suite 349
New York, NY 10003

© 2016 Brown Bear Books Ltd

For Brown Bear Books Ltd:
Editorial Director: Lindsey Lowe
Managing Editor: Tim Cooke
Children's Publisher: Anne O'Daly
Design Manager: Keith Davis
Designer: Melissa Roskell
Picture Manager: Sophie Mortimer

Picture Credits: Front Cover: Australian News and Information Service. Alamy: Chronicle 19; Art Gallery of South
Australia: 7; Atlas of NSW: 6; Australian News and Information Service: 28, 33, 39; Benalla Museum: 10; Dreamstime:
Alys Sand 5; Gold Museum Collection, Ballarat: 12; Ian Potter Museum: 13; Library of Congress: 31; Mary Evans Picture
Library: 17; David Moreno: 15; National Archives of Australia: 27, 35, 38, 41, 44; Ned Kelly Death of a Legend: 20; NSW
Tourism: 24, 26; pgstheway.com: 34; Public Record Office Victoria: 21; Ray White: 8; Robert Hunt Library: 4, 16, 29, 32,42;
Shutterstock: Jason Benz Bennee 22; State Library of Victoria, NSW: 9, 11, 23, 36, 37, 40, 45; Stringybark Creek Historic
Reserve: 18; Thinkstock: Photos.com 30; Topfoto: 25; Universal Pictures/Studio Canal: 43; Victoria Police Museum: 14.

Brown Bear Books has made every attempt to contact the copyright holder.
If anyone has any information please contact licensing@brownbearbooks.co.uk

Manufactured in the United States of America

CPSIA compliance information: Batch #CW16GS. For further information contact Gareth Stevens, New York, New York at 1-800-542-2595.

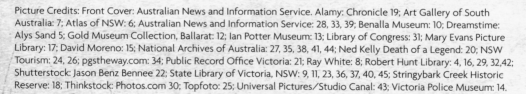

CONTENTS

INTRODUCTION

Ned Kelly was the most famous
outlaw in Australian history.
He committed numerous murders and
robberies but became a folk hero.

Ned Kelly was born to Irish parents in Victoria, southeast Australia, in either 1854 or 1855. At the time, Victoria was a colony ruled by Britain. Not many people lived there. As a young man Kelly became a horse and cattle thief. Later he and his brothers formed a gang. In 1878, the gang shot three policemen, who died. The Kelly Gang were declared **bushrangers**, or outlaws.

James Cook claims Australia for Britain on August 22, 1770. Settlers first arrived in 1787.

For the rest of his life Kelly was a wanted man. Despite his violent crimes, many Australians thought Kelly was a hero. Like him, they did not trust the British governors of Australia.

Life in Australia

When Ned Kelly was born in the 1850s, Australia was changing. Growing numbers of Europeans lived there. After Britain claimed Australia in 1770, it had used its new territory as somewhere to send its convicted criminals, or convicts. The first colonies in Australia were **penal colonies**. Most of the convicts had committed minor crimes such as theft. Many convicts stayed on in Australia after they had completed their prison sentence. The first free settlers began making the long journey to Australia in 1823.

Port Arthur was a British penal colony in what is now the Australian island of Tasmania. The colony had prison buildings and a large area of land farmed by convicts.

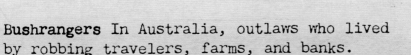

Bushrangers In Australia, outlaws who lived by robbing travelers, farms, and banks.

Penal colonies Remote settlements set up to hold prisoners.

The new settlers and former convicts found work as carpenters, farmers, and shepherds. Women worked as nurses or servants. Europeans lived mainly near the coast. They did not go into the Australian **bush**, where **aboriginal** peoples lived.

A growing country

In 1851 gold was discovered in Bathurst, New South Wales. This started a gold rush. The next year, 370,000 immigrants arrived in Australia to try to make their fortunes. Unlike earlier settlers, these gold diggers settled in inland parts of Australia. In 1853, Britain stopped sending its convicts to Australia. They were worried that people would commit a crime so they could be sent to Australia for free. That way they would be able to join the gold rush without paying for a ticket on a ship.

The gold rush began a period of modernization in Australia. In Victoria, where Ned Kelly was born, railroads spread out from the city of Melbourne. Melbourne itself was a busy port, with churches, theaters, and music halls.

This painting from about 1850 shows a meeting between white settlers and an aboriginal family. In reality, meetings between the two groups of people were often hostile or violent.

Ned's family was Irish, and his father was a former convict. Like many other Europeans in Australia, the Kellys believed the government protected wealthy landowners, known as squatters, rather than ordinary settlers. Ned Kelly's suspicion of authority soon led him into a life of crime.

Bush A large uninhabited area.

Aboriginal Describes people who have lived in a region since the earliest times.

Ned's Childhood

Edward "Ned" Kelly was born in Beveridge, Victoria. No one knows his exact birth date.

This is the house where Ned Kelly was born in Beveridge, Victoria, Australia.

Edward's father was an Irishman named John "Red" Kelly. He had been sent to Australia as a convict by the British after he had been found guilty of stealing pigs. Red Kelly was released from prison after seven years. He settled in Victoria and married a free Irish settler named Ellen Quinn.

Like many Irish people, the Kellys resented British rule in Ireland. Red and Ellen also believed the British authorities treated Irish settlers in Australia unfairly. Edward was the oldest of the eight Kelly children. He was always known as Ned.

A poor family

Ned worshipped his father. Red Kelly struggled to support his family on their farm in Beveridge. Ned's father and uncles began stealing cattle and horses to make a living. When Ned was about 10 years old, his father was sentenced to six months' **hard labor** for theft. After his release, Red began drinking. He died less than a year later. Ellen Kelly moved her family to a remote hut at Eleven Mile Creek in northern Victoria. They lived illegally on land that belonged to a wealthy landowner.

RED KELLY

Red Kelly was a huge influence on his eldest son. Ned Kelly greatly admired his father. Ned believed his father's death was caused by his time in prison. Ned thought his father had been picked on by the British. Red's death made Ned determined to rebel against the British authorities.

This police photograph shows Ned Kelly in around 1871. He was about 16 years old.

Hard labor Compulsory physical work carried out by prisoners as part of their sentence.

Trouble with the Law

After Red Kelly died, the young Ned found another father figure. He was an outlaw named Harry Power.

Ned Kelly wore this green sash beneath his armor in his last shootout with the police.

Ned became a local hero when he saved a young boy named Dick Shelton from drowning. The Shelton family were relatively well off. They gave Ned an emerald green **sash** to thank him for his bravery in saving their son. The sash became Ned's most prized possession. He later wore it during the robberies he carried out.

A slide into crime

In 1869, Ned was arrested. He was accused of attacking a Chinese man. He was held in prison for 10 days but then the case was dismissed. Meanwhile a bushranger named Harry Power arrived at the Kelly home in Eleven Mile Creek. He was an escaped convict. He taught Ned how to steal horses and in 1870 Ned was arrested and put in jail for helping Power steal horses. After seven weeks the charge was dropped.

First prison term

That same year, when he was about 15 years old, Ned spent six months in Beechworth Town jail for disturbing the peace. Soon after his release, he was sentenced to three years in jail for stealing another horse. When Ned was finally released he left Victoria and spent the next year traveling around Australia. He was poor, but managed to stay out of trouble for a while.

HARRY POWER

Harry Power was an Irish convict. He was sent to Australia from Ireland in 1840. He was freed, but was soon sent to prison again. In 1869 he escaped and became a bushranger. Ned Kelly helped him steal horses. In 1870 Power was arrested again and this time spent 15 years in jail.

The authorities in Victoria recruited aboriginal policemen to track bushrangers.

The first bushrangers were convicts who escaped to the bush during the early settlement of Australia.

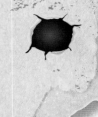

A bushranger talks to his aboriginal neighbors in the bush.

The first bushranger was John "Black" Caesar. He arrived in Australia with the first group of convicts in 1788. Caesar escaped from his penal colony and went to live in the bush. Other convicts soon followed him. The authorities usually let them go. They figured the convicts would die soon anyway.

The bolters

The bushrangers were known as "bolters." They stole food from other settlers to stay alive. Some of these men were violent criminals and murderers.

Over time, however, most bushrangers gained a romantic **reputation**. They became thought of as Australia's version of Robin Hood. Robin Hood had been a medieval outlaw in England who was said to have stolen from the rich in order to give to the poor. Although bushrangers usually stole for themselves, some did share the money from their robberies with the poor.

Local heroes

By the time Ned was born, there were fewer bushrangers than there had been before. The police were getting better at catching them. But bushrangers were still popular among poor rural settlers. They regarded the bushrangers as being brave men fighting against British injustice.

BUSHRANGERS' HEYDAY

The most profitable era for the bushrangers came in the 1850s and 1860s. It was the time of the gold rush. The bushrangers robbed travelers who were transporting their gold from remote goldfields to sell in towns. Gold was not only valuable. It was also easy to exchange for cash.

This painting shows bushrangers robbing travelers in southern Australia.

Reputation How someone or something is judged by other people.

Falsely Accused

When Ned returned home to Victoria in 1876, he learned that his mother had married a Californian, George King.

Constable Alexander Fitzpatrick said Ned Kelly tried to kill him, but no one knows if his story was true.

George King was a **rustler**. Ned Kelly went to work with his stepfather. Over the next three years, Ned, King, and their friends Joe Byrne and Aaron Sherritt stole around 280 horses. Local landowners wanted them to be stopped.

On April 15, 1878, a police constable named Alexander Fitzpatrick arrived at the Kelly home. He had come to arrest Ned's younger brother, Dan, for cattle stealing. He also hoped to invite Ned's sister, Kate, out on a date.

What happened next is unclear. Fitzpatrick said Dan Kelly resisted arrest and escaped and that Ned had tried to shoot him. The Kellys said his account was false. Ned Kelly said he was 200 miles (320 km) away at the time. Despite this, Ned was charged with attempted murder. A reward was offered for the capture of Ned and Dan Kelly.

Ellen arrested

When the police returned to Eleven Mile Creek to arrest the Kellys, the brothers were nowhere to be seen. Instead the police arrested their mother, Ellen Kelly. Judge Redmond Barry sentenced her to three years' hard labor. Barry said he would have sentenced Ned to 15 years in jail if Ned had been the one on trial.

This chimney is all that remains of the house at Eleven Mile Creek, where Fitzpatrick claimed he was attacked by Ned Kelly.

POLICE HARASSMENT?

The Kelly family saw themselves as victims of police harassment. They said Fitzpatrick's story showed that the police were picking on them. However, the Kellys were involved in stealing horses and cattle. The police wanted to put a stop to their illegal actions.

Rustler Someone who steals horses or cattle.

On the Run

Ned's mother was in jail and there
was a reward for Ned's capture.
He went into hiding with his brother
Dan and two of their friends.

Ned formed the Kelly Gang with his brother, Dan (1861–1880) and their friends, Joe Byrne (1856–1880) and Steve Hart (1859–1880). Both Byrne and Hart came from Irish families. They had looked up to Ned since they were young.

Ned was the undisputed leader of the gang. Dan was quite nervous and his behavior was sometimes unpredictable, but he was devoted to Ned. Hart was a brilliant horseman. Byrne was quiet. He was the brains behind the gang. Ned trusted Byrne more than he trusted anyone else.

Bushrangers wearing masks rob a coach. Ned decided he did not want to rob individuals.

This illustration shows one gangmember using a cave as a hideout in a remote part of Victoria.

Hideout in Victoria

The Kelly gang headed for the Wombat Ranges in Victoria. They found an old gold prospector's hut to use as a **hideout**. They strengthened its walls to make them bulletproof. The gang hid there for several months. Local people gave them food.

Meanwhile, the police had started to look for the gang. They soon realized that many people **sympathized** with the gang. People were helping Ned, Dan, and his friends stay hidden.

POLICE INEFFICIENCY

The police force in Victoria was not well organized. It had few men. It made little progress in tracking and catching the Kelly Gang. The police blamed the reason for this on the public's support for the gang. But this was probably just an excuse for their own inefficiency.

Hideout A safe place used to hide from other people.

Sympathized Shared the same feelings as someone else.

Killing at Stringybark Creek

The Kelly Gang had been in hiding for six months when, in October 1878, four policemen rode out to look for them.

The scene of the shootings at Stringybark Creek is now a peaceful public picnic site.

The policemen were Sergeant Michael Kennedy and Constables Thomas McIntyre, Michael Scanlan, and Thomas Lonigan. They hired an expert **tracker** to trace the Kelly Gang. The tracker led the policemen to Stringybark Creek in the Wombat Ranges. The four officers made a camp there. Unknown to them, their camp was just over a mile (1.6 km) from the Kelly Gang's hideout.

The police act

Two of the policemen began to look for the gang while the other two remained at the camp. Days passed with no sighting of Ned, Dan, or their friends. The policemen grew bored. On October 26, 1878, one of them started shooting at passing **cockatoos** for fun. The Kelly Gang heard the noise of the gunfire echoing around the creek. Realizing that the police were nearby, Ned Kelly decided to take action.

Shootout

The Kelly Gang crept up on the policemen's camp. Only Lonigan and McIntyre were there. Ned surprised them, while the other

In this drawing, Ned Kelly shoots Thomas Lonigan while the rest of the gang hold back Thomas McIntyre.

Tracker Someone who follows a trail left by animals or people.

Cockatoos Colorful birds of the parrot family.

members of the Kelly Gang hid in the bush nearby. There are different versions of what happened next. In one story, Ned said that he would let Lonigan and McIntyre go if they promised to **resign** from the police force. Kelly told them that if they did not keep their promise he would find them and kill them.

However, just as Ned was about to let them go, Scanlan and Kennedy returned. Lonigan shouted a warning that Kelly was in the camp. Ned shot Lonigan dead. The rest of the Kelly Gang came out of hiding. When Scanlan and Kennedy refused to surrender, Ned also shot them dead. Meanwhile, Thomas McIntyre managed to escape.

The gravestone of Sergeant Michael Kennedy. The Victoria police remembered their dead colleagues as heroes.

Another story

Another version of the story suggests that Thomas Lonigan drew his revolver as soon as Ned walked into the camp. Ned shot him dead at once. When the two other policemen returned, Scanlan tried to draw his gun, so Kelly shot him. Kennedy tried to run away, but Ned chased him and killed him.

ERECTED
by the
Parliament of Victoria
to the
Memory of
POLICE-SERGEANT
MICHAEL KENNEDY,
NATIVE OF WESTMEATH, IRELAND.
AGED 36 YEARS,
Who was
CRUELLY MURDERED BY ARMED CRIMINALS,
IN THE WOMBAT RANGES NEAR MANSFIELD
ON THE 26TH OCTOBER, 1878.
HE DIED IN THE SERVICE OF HIS COUNTRY,
OF WHICH HE WAS AN ORNAMENT,
HIGHLY RESPECTED BY ALL GOOD CITIZENS, AND
A TERROR TO EVIL-DOERS.

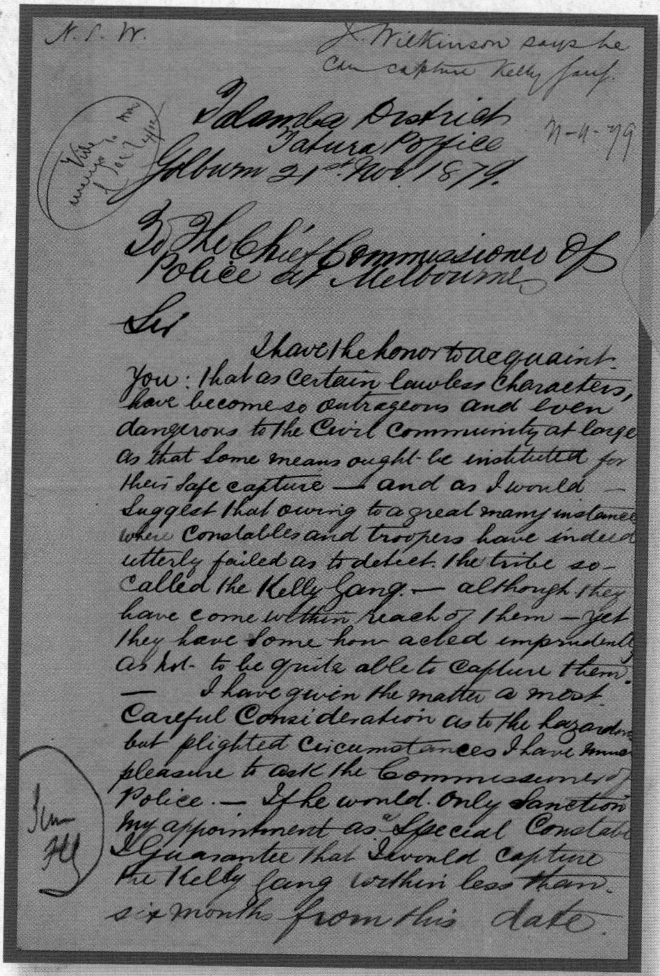

[Handwritten letter in cursive:]

Idamba District
Tatura Post Office
Golburn 21st Nov. 1879

To the Chief Commissioner of
Police at Melbourne

Sir

I have the honor to acquaint
You: that as certain lawless characters,
have become so outrageous and even
dangerous to the Civil community at large
as that some means ought be instituted for
their safe capture — and as I would
suggest that owing to a great many instances
when Constables and troopers have indeed
utterly failed as to detect the tribe so-
called the Kelly Gang. — although they
have come within reach of them — yet
they have some how acted imprudently
as not to be quite able to capture them.
— I have given the matter a most
Careful Consideration as to the hazardous
but plighted Circumstances I have immense
pleasure to ask the Commissioner of
Police. — If he would only sanction
my appointment as Special Constable
I Guarantee that I would capture
the Kelly Gang within less than
six months from this date.

> This account of the three killings was written by Constable McIntyre, the only police survivor.

Reporting the crime

Thomas McIntyre jumped on a horse. He rode to the nearby town of Mansfield where he reported the killings. The Kelly Gang was now wanted for killing three policemen. The Victoria police were determined not to let them get away with it.

WANTED DEAD OR ALIVE

The murders by the gang at Stringybark Creek marked a new level of crime for the Kelly Gang. They had killed three policemen and left nine children without fathers. The financial reward for the capture or death of members of the gang was increased and they were declared to be outlaws.

Resign To officially give up a job or government position.

The Outlaw Act

Just five days after the murders at Stringybark Creek, the British government of Victoria took action.

The government of Victoria was based in Parliament House in Melbourne.

As a direct result of the killings of the policemen, the government of Victoria introduced the Felons Apprehension Act on October 30, 1878. The act became law on November 1.

The Felons Apprehension Act

The act introduced the idea of being an outlaw to Australia. Anyone who had been issued with an arrest **warrant** no longer had the protection of the law. That meant that they could be stopped at any time and shot on sight, not only by the police but by anyone. The act also made it an offense to offer any help to an outlaw. Anyone who did so could be sent to jail.

V. R.

MURDER

OF POLICE.

£2,500 REWARD

WHEREAS, by a notice published in the *Government Gazette* bearing date the 30th October 1878, a Reward of FIVE HUNDRED POUNDS was offered by the Government for such information as would lead to the capture of each of the four men therein described charged with the murder of certain members of the Police Force, in the King River District: AND WHEREAS it is decided to increase the Reward for the apprehension of one of the said four offenders, named EDWARD KELLY, from FIVE HUNDRED POUNDS to ONE THOUSAND POUNDS: NOTICE IS HEREBY GIVEN that a Reward of ONE THOUSAND POUNDS will be paid by the Government for such information as will lead to the capture of the said EDWARD KELLY and FIVE HUNDRED POUNDS for each of the other three offenders referred to in the said notice of 30th October last.

This notification is in lieu of that of the 30th day of October 1878 above referred to, which is hereby cancelled.

GRAHAM BERRY,
Chief Secretary.

Chief Secretary's Office,
Melbourne, 13th December 1878.

BY AUTHORITY: JOHN FERRES, GOVERNMENT PRINTER, MELBOURNE.

The government advertised the reward offered for the capture of Ned and the rest of the gang. The amount of £2,500 in 1878 equals about $330,000 in today's money.

Surrender!

On November 4, 1878, the government in Victoria put up posters. They called on Ned and Dan Kelly to give themselves up by presenting themselves to the Mansfield Courthouse by November 12. The posters listed the other members of the gang as "unknowns." The courthouse stayed open to receive Ned and Dan. But they never turned up. On November 15, 1878, the Kelly Gang were declared outlaws. They were now on the run from anyone who wanted to catch them.

AN OUTLAW

Ned Kelly saw being declared an outlaw as a badge of honor. He thought it proved he was a victim of British injustice. He was proud of his new status. He later described himself as "a widow's son outlawed."

Warrant A legal document giving the police permission to arrest someone or to search a location.

Bank Robbers

Ned Kelly wanted to be a new kind of bushranger. He would only steal from the police and the banks. He wanted to make the gang famous.

The Old National Bank robbed by the Kelly Gang still stands in Euroa, Victoria.

On December 10, 1878, the Kelly Gang robbed the National Bank in Euroa. They cut telegraph wires to prevent the alarm from going off. They held the bank manager's wife **hostage** during the robbery. The gang got away with £2,000 in cash (about $264,000 in today's money) and 30 ounces (850 g) of gold. They also took all the bank's **mortgage** papers. These papers listed how much money people owed the bank. Without these records, the bank could not force people to pay. Many locals no longer had to pay their debts.

The Jerilderie raid

The gang's next bank robbery in Jerilderie on February 10, 1879, was even more daring. This time, the Kelly Gang locked up the local police and took their uniforms to wear as a disguise. They also locked the town's 30 inhabitants out of the way in the Royal Mail Hotel.

As the gang left town, they cut the telegraph wires to prevent news of the raid spreading across the country. But soon everyone was to hear about the Jerilderie raid.

FOOLING THE POLICE

The Jerilderie raid was embarrassing for the local police. The Kelly Gang locked up two policemen in the cells and stole their uniforms. They told everyone that they were "special constables." The Victoria police became even more determined to catch the Kelly Gang.

The Kelly Gang surprise the local police in Jerilderie before stealing their uniforms.

Hostage Someone who is held captive until certain conditions are met.

Mortgage A loan that is paid back in installments.

A Letter from Ned

After the public shame of the Jerilderie raid for the police, they had another shock waiting for them.

When the Kelly Gang left Jerilderie in February 1879, Ned left behind a long letter. He had **dictated** the letter to Joe Byrne. The handwritten letter was about 8,000 words long and covered 56 pages of notepaper.

The Jerilderie Letter

Ned used the letter to try to explain the reasons for his crimes. He described all the important events of his life. The letter explained Ned's side of the story about the day Sergeant Fitzpatrick was injured at the Kelly family home. Ned also gave his version of the killings at Stringybark Creek. Ned ended his letter by saying that he hoped the authorities would forgive him, but that he realized they would not because he had killed the policemen.

Public champion

In his letter, Ned also tried to claim that he was fighting for social change in Victoria. He said that landowners known as squatters had grabbed much of the best land during the early settlement of the colony. Many citizens in Victoria resented this **elite**, which they called the "squattocracy." Ned's letter demanded that the squatters should be forced to share their land with the poor.

A WIDER AUDIENCE

Ned Kelly wanted his letter to be printed in the newspaper for everyone to read. The local newspaper editor, Samuel Gill, had escaped during the robbery, so Ned instead left the letter with Edwin Living, the accountant of the Jerilderie bank. Living promised to ask Gill to print the letter. However, the letter did not appear in print until 1930, long after Ned's death.

Ned Kelly had dictated the letter to Joe Byrne some months before the raid on the bank at Jerilderie.

Dictated Said aloud for someone else to write down.

Elite A small group of people seen as being superior to everyone else.

Public Sympathy

Ned wanted to give the impression that his gang were ordinary people. He claimed the police had caused them to become criminals by treating them unfairly.

After the Jerilderie bank raid, the Kelly Gang spent the rest of 1879 and early 1880 in hiding. But although they were out of the public eye, the popularity of the gang grew. People admired the gang's claim to be fighting injustice. Many citizens shared the view that the police were **corrupt** and inefficient. The public did not give the police any information about the Kelly Gang.

Many Australians thought Ned Kelly was a hero. They thought he was standing up to the police.

Police response

The local police decided to take action. They arrested many of Ned's acquaintances. Around 300 police and soldiers flooded into the local towns to look for the gang. The reward money offered for the capture of

the gang was also raised to £8,000 (about $1,085,000 in today's money). This was a huge sum at the time, yet it seemed that no one had any information to give the police.

With so many police and soldiers trying to hunt down the gang, some men started to act on their own, rather than as a unit, hoping to claim the reward money. Efforts to catch the Kelly Gang were in **disarray**.

A FAIR CRIMINAL

Ned was determined that the public did not think of his gang as criminals. He wanted to be seen as a champion of the poor farmers living in the bush. Kelly destroyed their mortgage documents when he raided banks. That released farmers from their debts. The gang never raided people's homes or farms.

Corrupt Acting dishonestly in return for money or other forms of reward.

Disarray A lack of order or organization.

Focus: Folk Heroes

Ned Kelly was not the first outlaw to become a folk hero. Criminals at other times had also attracted sympathy and public support.

Robin Hood became the model for outlaws who claimed to be fighting against injustice.

Outlaws have often been admired for seeming to stand up for ordinary people against an unfair government. The outlaws justified their crimes in this way, as Ned Kelly did in the Jerilderie Letter. These outlaws claimed their crimes were against injustice in society, not against ordinary citizens.

In the 1860s, for example, an Australian bushranger named Frank Gardiner (c. 1830– c. 1904) was accused of stealing a poor man's money and boots. Gardiner wrote to a newspaper to deny that he would do such a thing. Gardiner compared himself to Robin Hood, who was said to be an outlaw in medieval England. No one knows if Robin Hood actually existed, but he featured in legends and **ballads**. His gang was said to rob from the rich to give to the poor.

Jesse James thought of himself as being a champion of the Southern states against the government in Washington, D.C.

America's Robin Hoods

Other outlaws who compared themselves with Robin Hood included the American bank robber Jesse James (1847–1882). James was popular because people saw him as standing up to an unpopular government. The famous American gunfighter Billy the Kid (1859–1881) was also popular in the American West. People saw him as fighting for ordinary citizens against powerful ranchers who controlled the Western states.

★★★
THE HIGHWAYMEN

In the 17th and 18th centuries many Britons saw **highwaymen** as folk heroes. These robbers on horseback held up travelers. They were seen as brave men who usually did not harm their victims. At his trial in 1696 the highwayman Henry Bliss said "The poor I fed, the rich I sent empty away." The most famous highwayman was Dick Turpin (c. 1705–1739).

Ballads Long poems or songs that tell a story.

Highwaymen Robbers on horseback who held up travelers in order to seize their possessions.

Death of an Informer

As the hunt for the Kelly gang continued, the police questioned Aaron Sherritt. Sherritt was an old friend of Joe Byrne.

Aaron Sherritt wears his hat strap under his nose. This was a fashionable look for the Greta Mob, a young gang to which Dan Kelly also belonged.

Aaron Sherritt (1855–1880) had helped Ned, Joe, and George King steal horses in 1876. Now he told the gang what the police had found out about them. But Ned feared Sherritt had switched sides and was passing information about the gang to the police.

A test

The gang decided to test Ned's theory. They set a trap for Sherritt. They told Sherritt's mother that they were planning to kill Sherritt. The police immediately gave Sherritt special protection. For the Kelly Gang, this seemed to be proof that Sherritt was an **informer**.

Joe Byrne worked out a real plan to murder Sherritt. On June 26, 1880, he forced another friend of Sherritt's to go with him to Sherritt's home. At gunpoint, he made the friend call out for Aaron Sherritt. When Sherritt opened the door of his house, Byrne killed him. He allowed the other friend to live. Four policemen were supposed to be protecting Sherritt. They had all taken cover under the bed when they heard the gunshots.

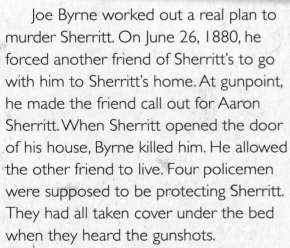

JOE BYRNE

Joe Byrne was the man Ned trusted the most. After Ned chose the gang's targets, it was Byrne who planned how to carry out the robberies. Byrne had been to school and had grown up on the goldfields during the Gold Rush. Byrne also spoke Chinese as a result of living with Chinese gold diggers.

Informer Someone who gives information about someone else to the police.

Operation at Glenrowan

In June 1880, the Kelly Gang's criminal activities were to come to a dramatic end at the small railroad stop of Glenrowan.

Ned Kelly and his gang held the citizens hostage in the Glenrowan Hotel, which was the largest building in town.

Glenrowan was on the railroad between Melbourne and Beechworth. On June 27, 1880, the day after Sherritt's murder, Ned Kelly and Steve Hart removed a small section of railroad track on a dangerous bend just outside the town. They rode into town and rounded up the 62 townspeople.

No ordinary raid

The captives were held in the town's hotel for the rest of the day and through the night. The mood was a little like a party. There was music, dancing, and games to pass the time. Ned Kelly knew that news of the **siege** would bring the police to Glenrowan.

The police would arrive by train, which would be traveling fast when it reached the missing section of track. Ned planned for the train to **derail**. He wanted to kill the police in revenge for Sherritt's treachery.

Ned was right. The police sent a train, but it was late arriving at Glenrowan. As they waited, the Kelly Gang grew nervous. One of Ned's prisoners was the schoolmaster, Thomas Curnow. He asked Ned to let him leave the hotel. When Ned agreed, Curnow rushed to the railroad. He walked down the track waving his sister's red scarf so he could be seen. Curnow stopped the train before it reached the damaged track.

THE GANG'S PRISONERS

The Kelly Gang treated the hostages at Glenrowan well. Some were allowed to come and go from the hotel. Ned Kelly did not want the gang to be known for harming ordinary Australians. He let Thomas Curnow go because Curnow claimed he needed to look after his wife, who he said was sick.

Police surround the hotel at Glenrowan in this drawing from the time.

Siege The act of surrounding a place so that no people or goods can get in or out.

Derail For a train to come off the tracks.

Final Shootout

Having escaped Ned Kelly's trap, the police made their way to Glenrowan for a final confrontation with the Kelly Gang.

Wearing his homemade metal armor, Ned Kelly approaches the police for the final shootout.

Early on the morning of Monday, June 28, 1880, the Kelly Gang prepared to fight it out with the police. The outlaws put on special homemade armor. Meanwhile the police surrounded the Glenrowan Hotel.

The gang and police began shooting at one another. After about 15 minutes, smoke from the guns made it impossible to see anything. The firing stopped. The police waited for **reinforcements**. Meanwhile, the Kelly Gang allowed women and children to leave the hotel unharmed.

Ned appears

Ned came out of the hotel. He was wearing armor that covered his head and upper body. The police shot at him, but the bullets bounced off the metal, so the police shot him in his legs. Ned fell to the ground and was surrounded by police. He knew the game was up.

Meanwhile, inside the hotel, Joe Byrne was hit by a stray bullet and died. Soon afterward, Steve Hart and Dan Kelly were also shot dead in the hotel. The police set fire to the damaged building. It burned to the ground. The notorious Kelly Gang had been defeated.

THE GANG'S ARMOR

The Kelly Gang wore homemade armor at Glenrowan. They used the metal from plow blades. They beat the blades together. The armor weighed 97 pounds (44 kg). It covered the entire upper bodies and heads of the outlaws. Their legs and arms, however, were left unprotected.

Having been shot in the legs, Kelly lies on the ground surrounded by police officers.

Reinforcements Extra personnel who increase the numbers of a force.

37

On Trial

Ned was the sole survivor of the Kelly Gang. He was taken to Melbourne and put on trial for the murders of Kennedy, Lonigan, and Scanlan at Stringybark Creek.

This drawing shows the scene in the courtroom. Many Australians read about the trial in the newspapers.

Ned's trial took place on October 28, 1880, in the state capital of Melbourne. The authorities chose Melbourne deliberately. Unlike people in the bush, people in the city of Melbourne had no sympathy for the Kelly Gang. The trial judge was Sir Redmond Barry. He was the same man who had sent Ned's mother to jail in 1878.

An expected outcome

The first charge was the murder of Constable Lonigan. Ned pleaded not guilty, but the outcome of the trial was never in doubt. Barry told the jury they must either find Kelly guilty of murder or **acquit** him. The jury was not able to find him guilty of any charge other than murder. It took just half an hour to return a guilty verdict. Ned Kelly was sentenced to death.

At the end of the trial, Ned promised Judge Barry that he would see the judge soon after death. Strangely, Barry died just 12 days after Ned was executed.

JUDGE REDMOND BARRY

Redmond Barry (1813–1880) was born in County Cork, Ireland. He moved to Sydney, Australia, in 1837 and became a lawyer. He became the first chancellor of the University of Melbourne and solicitor-general of Victoria. Barry died unexpectedly within two weeks of Ned Kelly's execution.

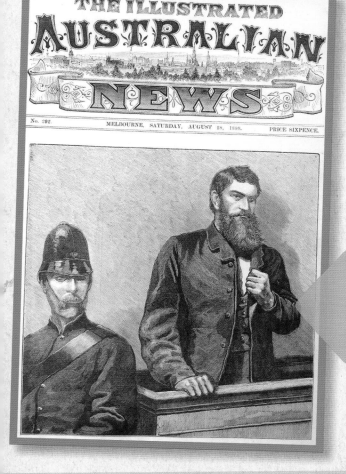

THE ILLUSTRATED AUSTRALIAN NEWS

No. 292.　　MELBOURNE, SATURDAY, AUGUST 28, 1880.　　PRICE SIXPENCE.

The Illustrated Australian News shows Ned Kelly speaking during his trial.

Death of Ned Kelly

On November 11, 1880, Ned Kelly was hanged in prison in Melbourne. He was just 25 years old.

Ned Kelly walks to the scaffold in this drawing of his hanging in the prison.

Before his execution, Ned was allowed to see members of his family. His mother was still a prisoner. She is said to have told him, "Mind you die like a Kelly." Ned spent his last few days writing long letters to the authorities. He complained about how badly poor Australians were treated by them. There were several public protests against Ned's death sentence. Up to 30,000 people signed a **petition** for the execution to be canceled.

Ned's execution

Just before the time for his execution, the chains were removed from Ned's legs. He was taken to a special room where he waited for a chaplain to arrive. After receiving the last rites, Kelly walked to the **scaffold**. Some newspapers claimed that Ned planned to make a speech before his death, but he did not. As the hangman's noose was placed over his head, he is supposed to have said, "Ah well, I suppose it has come to this."

After Ned had been hanged, a death mask of his face was cast. His body was buried in a mass grave at the prison in Melbourne.

COLLECTING THE REWARD

The reward for the capture of the Kelly Gang was split between many people, including the police at Glenrowan and Thomas Curnow, who had prevented the train wreck. The largest sum went to Superintendent Francis Hare, the police commander at Glenrowan. Hare received a share of the reward even though he was also suspended for cowardice when he left Glenrowan during the shootout after being slightly injured.

This plaster mask was made of Ned Kelly's face after his execution.

Petition A formal request for something signed by many people.

Scaffold A platform from which a criminal is hanged.

Focus: Ned's Legacy

Ned Kelly was famous in his lifetime. With his death, his reputation increasingly changed from notorious outlaw to popular folk hero.

THE STORY OF THE KELLY GANG

(By BIOGRAPH) Specially taken by Mᴱˢˢʳˢ JOHNSON & GIBSON, Melbourne.

An Entirely NEW and EXQUISITE Pictorial Representation of

The Thrilling Story of The KELLYS

In 1906 the story of Ned Kelly was the subject of the first feature film ever made in Australia.

Since his death in 1880, Ned Kelly's image has changed. In the late 19th century, the first written accounts of the bushrangers stressed the fact that they were violent criminals. The accounts did not suggest that the Kelly Gang were heroes.

More modern books, poems, and movies have often shown Kelly as a kind of modern-day Robin Hood, stealing from the rich and helping the poor. Some Australians have seen Ned's fight against the police as a **symbol** of the wider struggle against British rule.

The movie star

Ned Kelly was the subject of Australia's first full-length movie, *The Story of the Kelly Gang* (1906). Since then, Ned has been depicted in many movies. In 1970 he was played by Mick Jagger, lead singer in the British rock band The Rolling Stones.

In the 1940s the Australian artist Sidney Nolan painted a series of pictures of Ned Kelly. The paintings show Kelly as a symbol of the Australian rebel spirit. They are among the most popular Australian works of art ever created.

Heath Ledger (second from left) played Ned in the 2003 movie Ned Kelly. Orlando Bloom (third from left) played Joseph Byrne.

NED KELLY'S SKULL

In 1929 a skull was found during building work at the prison in Melbourne. The skull was marked with the initials EK. It almost certainly belonged to Ned, or Edward, Kelly. In the 1970s the skull was put on display. It was stolen in 1972, but recovered in 1978.

Symbol Something that represents something else.

ROGUES' GALLERY

Ned Kelly was the last and most famous of the bushrangers. There had been many other outlaws who fought the law in the Australian bush.

Dan Morgan
(c. 1830–1865)

"Mad" Dan Morgan was a bloodthirsty highway robber. He killed a number of people. After he killed a policeman a reward was put up for his capture or death. Morgan used his survival skills to stay free. He was shot and killed after he attacked and robbed the McPherson family at their farm in Victoria.

Ben Hall
(1837–1865)

Known as "Brave Ben," Hall carried out raids in New South Wales. He deliberately set out to annoy the police. Hall is not known to have killed anyone. He was shot dead by police in May 1865. The police claimed they acted under the Felons Apprehension Act of that year, but it had not been put into effect at the time.

The Clarke Brothers

Thomas (c. 1840–1867) and John (c. 1846–1867) were bushrangers in the goldfields of New South Wales. They were notorious for violence. During some 36 holdups, they killed at least five people. Their victims included policemen sent to track them down. The Clarke brothers were finally captured in March 1867. After being tried for murder, they were hanged in prison in Sydney.

Dan Kelly

(1861–1880)

Dan adored his older brother Ned. Like Ned, Dan was an excellent horseman. Also like his brother, Dan was in trouble with the police from an early age. Before he joined the Kelly Gang, Dan belonged to the Greta Mob. This gang was known for their unusual appearance. The gang had long hair. They wore their hats at an angle, held on by string that passed underneath their noses. The gang also wore colorful sashes around their waists.

GLOSSARY

Aboriginal Describes people who have lived in a region since the earliest times.

Acquit To find someone not guilty of a crime.

Ballads Long poems or songs that tell a story.

Bush A large uninhabited area.

Bushrangers In Australia, outlaws who lived by robbing travelers, farms, and banks.

Cockatoos Colorful birds of the parrot family.

Corrupt Acting dishonestly in return for money or other forms of reward.

Derail For a train to come off the tracks.

Dictated Said aloud for someone else to write down.

Disarray A lack of order or organization.

Elite A small group of people seen as being superior to everyone else.

Hard labor Compulsory physical work carried out by prisoners as part of their sentence.

Hideout A safe place used to hide from other people.

Highwaymen Robbers on horseback who held up travelers in order to seize their possessions.

Hostage Someone who is held captive until certain conditions are met.

Informer Someone who gives information about someone to the police.

Mortgage A loan that is paid back in installments.

Penal colonies Remote settlements set up to hold prisoners.

Petition A formal request for something signed by many people.

Reinforcements Extra personnel who increase the numbers of a force.

Reputation How someone or something is judged by other people.

Resign To officially give up a job or government position.

Rustler Someone who steals horses or cattle.

Sash A band worn around the waist or over the shoulder.

Scaffold A platform from which a criminal is hanged.

Siege The act of surrounding a place so that no people or goods can get in or out.

Symbol Something that represents something else.

Sympathized Shared the same feelings as someone else.

Tracker Someone who follows a trail left by animals or people.

Warrant A legal document giving the police permission to arrest someone or search a location.

FURTHER RESOURCES

Books

Bingham, Jane. *Living in the Australian Outback*. World Cultures. Chicago, IL: Raintree Perspectives, 2007.

Boxer, Charlie. *Ned Kelly: Gangster Hero of the Australian Outback*. Who Was? London, UK: Short Books, 2004.

Lindop, Christine. *Ned Kelly: A True Story*. Oxford Bookworms Library. New York: Oxford University Press, 2008.

Turner, Kate. *Australia*. Countries of the World. Washington, DC: National Geographic Society, 2007.

Websites

http://www.australia.gov.au/about-australia/australian-story/ned-kelly
A page from the Australian government about Ned Kelly's life and his status as an Australian folk hero.

http://www.ironoutlaw.com/
A comprehensive privately maintained site about all elements of Ned Kelly's life and times.

http://nga.gov.au/Nolan/Index.cfm
The National Gallery of Australia's introduction to Sidney Nolan's series of paintings of Ned Kelly, with a link to the complete gallery.

http://www.bbc.com/news/magazine-21077457
An article from the British Broadcasting Corporation about how Ned Kelly's reputation still divides Australians.

http://www.australiangeographic.com.au/topics/history-culture/2011/09/ned-kelly-timeline
A timeline of Ned Kelly's life from *Australian Geographic* magazine.

Publisher's note to educators and parents: Our editors have carefully reviewed these websites to ensure that they are suitable for students. Many websites change frequently, however, and we cannot guarantee that a site's future contents will continue to meet our high standards of quality and educational value. Be advised that students should be closely supervised whenever they access the Internet.

INDEX